TEDDY'S SPACE ADVENTURE

"IT REALLY HAPPENED!"

WRITTEN BY **JAN DUFFY** & **SHANNON DUFFY PAYNE**

ILLUSTRATED BY **AUTUMN POTTER**

With special thanks to:

Brian Duffy

Shaun P. Duffy

Adam A. Brown

for their invaluable edits and support.

Their contributions made this book possible.

A little girl named Shannon with curly red hair and freckles met her first teddy
bear and it was love at first sight. She knew the bear's name at once,
as it was sewn neatly on a crisp white tag that peeked out
from the perfect stitching on its soft brown fur...
"Teddy!" Shannon squealed with delight.

"Teddy, now we can experience all of life's adventures together!" Shannon declared.

How wonderful! thought Teddy. Although unsure what adventures might come, Teddy was thrilled that they had found each other.

Shannon and Teddy loved spending their days together.

They laughed and played everywhere they went.

Shannon's dad was a pilot in the Air Force, so the family had to move often, and Teddy was always by her side.

When Shannon was three years old, her dad was selected to be an astronaut! Upon hearing the news, the family cheered and hugged.

Dad, Mom, Shannon, her older brother Shaun and Teddy too (of course!) packed up and moved to Houston, Texas, where astronauts trained. Teddy didn't know what an astronaut was but could see from the family's excitement that this would be their greatest adventure yet!

Before they knew it, Houston was home. Life went on as usual for Shannon and Teddy while Dad learned about the NASA Astronaut Program and began training for space flight.

Then one night, Dad gave Shannon a huge hug and announced, "Tomorrow is a big day, your first day of kindergarten! I'm sure Teddy will look forward to hearing all about your adventures at school."

"But can't Teddy come too?" Shannon asked softly, with a quivering lip. "Not this time," answered Dad in his comforting voice, "but think of how happy you'll be to see each other again when you get home." Shannon and Teddy held back tears as they each tried to imagine what a day without the other would be like.

In the beginning, it was hard for Shannon and Teddy to be apart during the day. Shannon made new friends at school but couldn't wait to share her stories with Teddy each evening. Teddy was eventually able to go to school with Shannon on show-and-tell and other special days. *I must be the luckiest teddy bear in the world!* thought Teddy, who could tell from Shannon's hugs and smiles that she also felt like the luckiest red-headed girl.

The days flew by as Shannon and Teddy kept busy going to soccer games with Dad, shopping with Mom and riding bikes with Shaun.

The family also found time to enjoy the many experiences Houston had to offer. They saw giraffes, tigers and elephants at the Zoo . . .

. . . watched cowboys, horses and live bands at the Houston Livestock Show & Rodeo . . .

. . . and cheered on their favorite baseball team, the Astros, at the Astrodome.

Most of all, Shannon and Teddy loved visiting Space Center Houston where they discovered the magic and wonder of exploring outer space.

On a day just like any other, Dad came home grinning from ear to ear with big news to share. "I'm going on my first Space Shuttle flight next year!"

The family again celebrated with a big group hug, and this time added some high-fives!

With Dad's flight assignment now official, the family traveled to Florida to experience a Space Shuttle launch in person, so they could all know what to expect when it was Dad's turn.

The event was unlike any other. As the clock counted down to zero, Shannon felt the ground shake, saw the sky light up and heard the roar of the rocket as it left the earth. Shannon and Teddy clutched each other tightly, knowing that the next time they watched a launch, Dad would be riding the rocket, not standing safely within their reach.

The family returned to Houston more nervous and excited for Dad's mission. His training intensified as the countdown to liftoff shortened from months, to weeks, to days.

MARCH

FEB

At last, it was time for Dad's first launch. A week before the launch date, he had to begin quarantine with his crew members to protect them from getting sick. When Shannon and Dad hugged goodbye, her eyes filled up with tears. Dad could see she was nervous, and in his comforting way, he reassured her, "Don't worry, sweetie – I'll see you soon. And you'll have Teddy right by your side." Shannon gripped Teddy tighter than ever, already looking forward to the reunion with Dad after the flight.

Teddy thought of how brave Dad was to go on this adventure, then realized that they would need courage as well (even just staying on Earth!) while missing Dad and wondering whether he was alright.

The final days leading up to the launch were full of excitement. Mom, Shaun, Shannon and Teddy were supported by hundreds of family and friends gathered in Cape Canaveral, Florida, to watch the spectacular Shuttle liftoff.

They were able to catch glimpses of Dad (still in quarantine with the crew) on the NASA Select TV channel.

Shannon and Teddy stared in awe at the astronauts on the screen as they suited up in their flight suits, boarded a van, rode to the launch pad and finally climbed aboard the Space Shuttle.

Mom, Shaun, Shannon and Teddy held on to one another, bracing for blast off.

Shannon's eyes grew wide and her heart raced as the Shuttle left

the ground and began ascending into the sky.

She stood speechless, tears streaming

down her freckled face,

never letting go of Teddy.

After coming out of the initial shock,

Shannon joined in the celebration of a successful launch, clapping and cheering with

Mom, Shaun, Teddy and the other astronaut families.

The family returned to their lives in Houston, while Dad orbited the world about

200 miles above them. They knew he was busy, having almost every minute

planned according to a daily flight schedule, and they wondered if he was having

fun floating around in zero gravity. After all, this is what he had trained for and

looked forward to for so long.

Once the mission was over, the family was more than ready to get back to Florida and cheer on the Shuttle's landing. Though the landing would be much quieter than the launch, the families of the crew were still anxious for the moment they could see their loved ones again.

The small audience stared at the sky for any sign of the Shuttle. Shannon and Teddy both tried their hardest not to blink. In an instant, the black and white space vehicle seemed to appear out of nowhere and, in less than a minute, glided safely back to Earth. The family cried tears of joy when they all got to hug again.

Shannon had a thousand thoughts all at once, and even more questions, but managed only to say, "Dad, I missed you!" "I missed you too, sweetie!" he said, with a great big smile and hugs for her, Shaun, Mom and, of course, Teddy.

Over the next several years, Dad went on two more missions. The family, including Teddy, made the trips together to each of the launches and landings, and always felt just as nervous and excited.

2000
1999

As they watched Dad disappear into the sky above and return weeks later... the family shouted together, "Go, Dad, go!"

Go, Dad, Go!

Hee Hee

Even though Shannon and Teddy were never quite comfortable while Dad was off the planet, they had a bit of telephone fun. When anyone called for Dad, they answered, "He can't come to the phone right now, he's in space!" When the caller replied in disbelief, "Yeah right, kid," Shannon hung up and giggled with Teddy until they were out of breath!

By the time Dad was assigned to his fourth and final space flight, Shannon had grown from a little girl with curly red hair and freckles into a young adult. Teddy, too, showed signs of the years gone by, with faded brown fur and the once crisp white tag now frayed and worn.

Shannon spent less time at home and would no longer bring Teddy to school with her. Teddy still enjoyed hearing stories from Shannon's days, when Shannon wasn't too busy with homework, sports and social events. At times, Teddy longed to be part of the adventures again.

One evening at dinner, the family excitedly discussed the details of Dad's upcoming mission. The goal of the seven-member crew would be to help build the International Space Station (ISS). The ISS would allow future astronauts to live and work in space for months or even years at a time. Shannon was glad her dad would only be gone for a couple of weeks!

Then, Dad turned to Shannon and asked, "What would you think if I brought Teddy along this time?" Shannon was surprised by the question and suddenly remembered her first day of school, all those years ago when Dad told her she would have to leave Teddy home. Like then, she would miss Teddy, but she would be thrilled to hear all about the adventure when they reunited. Without further thought, Shannon blurted out, "Sure, Dad, that will be SO cool!"

Teddy was over the moon excited to have this chance, then quickly realized it was impossible to be on board the Space Shuttle and in Shannon's arms at the same time. How would she manage without her favorite bear right by her side? But Shannon seemed to know Teddy was concerned and said, "Don't worry, Teddy. I'll have Mom and Shaun to keep me company. Think of how much fun you'll have and how happy we'll be to see each other again when you get home!" Her comforting (and vaguely familiar) words immediately put Teddy at ease.

The pre-launch goodbye was tearful, as Shannon gave big hugs to both Dad and Teddy, who joined their fellow crew members in quarantine. Mom, Shaun and Shannon's trip to Florida felt strange this time, since Teddy wasn't with them.

As the family waited eagerly for liftoff, Dad was strapped into his seat on the Shuttle's flight deck, while Teddy was carefully tucked into a locker on the mid-deck. Shannon and Teddy each wondered how the other was feeling as the hour drew nearer for Teddy's ride of a lifetime!

Shannon held on tightly to Mom and Shaun as the countdown swiftly reached

10, 9, 8, 7, 6, 5, 4, 3, 2, 1, LIFTOFF!

All together, they shouted "Go, Dad, go!" followed by "Go, Teddy, go!"

After eight and a half fast and furious minutes, the Shuttle reached the stillness of outer space. Even at a speed of 17,500 miles per hour, the travel time for the Shuttle to the International Space Station was several days! As the Shuttle approached the ISS, Dad had to be very careful and exact with his steering to make sure the vehicles would come together just right.

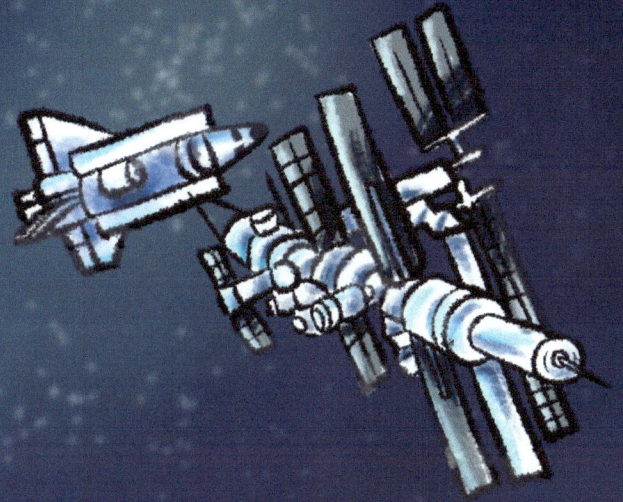

Upon docking with the Space Station, Dad safely removed Teddy so they could float together. Teddy loved being in zero gravity, suspended in mid-air. *How cool that there is no up or down!* Teddy thought, while wishing that Shannon could be there to experience the freedom of floating, too.

When it was time to open the hatch and enter the Space Station for the first time, Dad eagerly grabbed Teddy's arm and proclaimed, "Here we go!" He and Teddy glided through the docking tunnel into the Station.

It felt like a new home – so clean and bright! From the many windows, they could look down on the beautiful colors of Earth, which they circled every 90 minutes. Dad made sure to point out to Teddy when they were above Houston, and Teddy wondered if Shannon was looking up at the same time.

Shannon gazed up at the sky often, thinking about what Dad and Teddy were up to at that moment. She missed them both more than ever, but also felt at peace, knowing that they were together on this great space adventure.

While enjoying the new surroundings of the Space Station, Dad suddenly had the idea to spend the night on board. He grabbed his sleeping bag and invited all the crew members to join, but they preferred to rest aboard the familiar Shuttle. "Well, Teddy, it looks like it's just you and me tonight!" Dad said. With that, for the first time ever, a human and a teddy bear said "good night" aboard the ISS, all by themselves.

The seven-person (and one teddy bear) crew made the most of their remaining mission time. Teddy marveled at the astronauts living and working in space, and knew just what to share with Shannon first: you had to watch out for floating debris, or else you might collide with an escaped blob of mashed potatoes or macaroni and cheese while doing a somersault!

Spacewalk days were especially busy and exciting. First, one of the astronauts used the robotic arm to carefully pick up a piece of hardware from the Shuttle's payload bay and add it to the Space Station. Then, it was time for the spacewalkers to put on their bulky white suits and venture outside to finish the assembly. Teddy had a front row seat to observe every exhilarating moment.

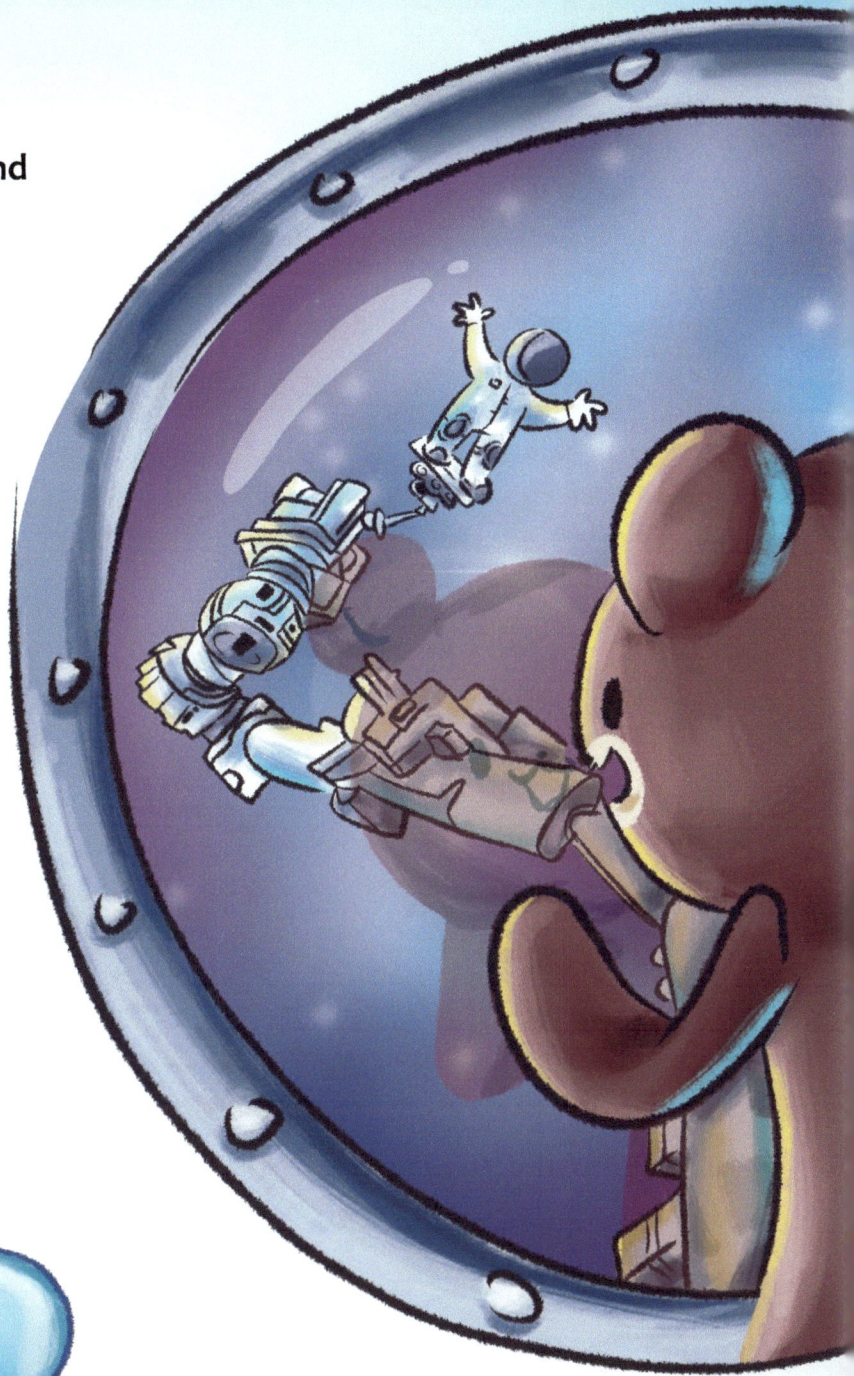

During the flight, the astronauts completed four spacewalks, fulfilling their mission to transform the Space Station into the first home away from Earth. With each exciting step completed, Teddy thought, *Shannon will love hearing all about this!*

When it was time to head home, the Shuttle undocked from the ISS, then Teddy, Dad and the crew returned to their pre-launch positions. While reflecting on the journey as the Shuttle descended toward Earth, Teddy thought, *I'm no longer the luckiest teddy bear in the world ... I'm the luckiest teddy bear in the universe!* With memories to last a lifetime, Teddy couldn't wait to return home and for the family to all be together again.

The reunions were always the best part, but this time was even more special for Shannon because it had been Dad's last flight and Teddy's greatest voyage (so far). She hugged them both as hard as she could, unable to stop the tears of happiness and relief at having them home.

Many years have passed, but Teddy and Shannon still enjoy sharing the memories and stories of their experiences. Their audience has grown, now that Shannon has three little redheads of her own, and their favorite story of all is (of course) Teddy's Space Adventure!

THE END

About the Authors

JAN DUFFY lives in Houston, Texas, with her husband Brian. They have 2 adult children, Shaun and Shannon, and 3 grandchildren. Shaun works as an engineer at Johnson Space Center. Jan holds degrees in education from Purdue University (BA) and The University of West Florida (M.Ed). She had a career teaching elementary school and is now retired. Jan always wanted to write a children's book, so when Brian took Shannon's teddy bear to space it seemed like the perfect story! Mother and daughter had fun in the process and hope you enjoy the story!

SHANNON DUFFY PAYNE earned her BBA from The University of Texas at Austin in 2005. Since graduating, she's worked in the financial services industry. Shannon currently lives in Houston with her husband, Thomas, whom she married in 2010. They have 3 children who keep them blissfully busy. In her occasional free time, Shannon enjoys watching sports (especially college football and tennis), jogging and spending time with family.

TEDDY resides in Houston with the family and enjoys snuggling, doing bear-obics to stay in shape, and living by the motto: "Nothing is im-pawsible, if you set your mind to it."

About the Illustrator

AUTUMN POTTER is an artist and animator. She enjoys watching cartoons, sewing and drawing. She has received the awards of State Champion of the 2021 UIL Young Filmmakers competition and State Finalist in the 2021 Visual Arts Scholastic Event. She hopes to follow the footsteps of Stephen Hillenburg and pursue animation.

About the Book

Shannon's father, **COLONEL BRIAN DUFFY**, USAF (Ret.), is a former astronaut who flew on 4 Space Shuttle missions. He is a graduate of the United States Air Force Academy, the University of Southern California and the USAF Test Pilot School. He was the pilot of STS-45 and 57 and commanded STS-72 and 92. He took his daughter's teddy bear (Teddy) to the International Space Station (ISS) on his final mission in October 2000. They are pictured above in the Russian segment of the ISS.

Shaun, Mom (Jan Duffy), Dad (Brian Duffy) and Shannon reunited after the landing of STS-72 (Dad's third mission) in January 1996.

Mom, Shaun, Shannon and Teddy anxiously awaited the safe return of Dad and the STS-72 crew in January 1996.

Shannon, Teddy, Shaun and Mom stood close together to watch the launch of STS-57 from the roof of the Launch Control Center in Cape Canaveral, Florida (June 1993).

www.ingramcontent.com/pod-product-compliance
Lightning Source LLC
Chambersburg PA
CBHW042029090426
42811CB00016B/1791

9 780578 355634